Home Remedies

(For Common Ailments with Easy Recipes)

TARLA DALAL

India's #1 Cookery Author

S&C

SANJAY & CO.

MUMBAI

Sixth Printing : 2011

Price: Rs.99/-

Published & Distributed by : **Sanjay & Company**

A-1/353, Shah & Nahar Industrial Estate, Dhanraj Mill Compound, Lower Parel (W), Mumbai - 400 013. INDIA.
Tel. : (91-22) 4345 2400 • Fax : (91-22) 2496 5876

For books, Membership on **tarladalal.com**, Subscription for **Cooking & More** and Recipe queries
Timing : 9.30 a.m. to 6.00 p.m., Monday to Friday, 9.30 a.m. to 1.00 p.m. Saturday
Contact : Tel. : (91-22) 4345 2400 • Fax : (91-22) 2496 5876
E-mail : ravindra@tarladalal.com • sanjay@tarladalal.com

Nutritionist	**Typesetting**	**Design**	**Printed by :**
Nisha Katira	Adityas Enterprises	Satyamangal Rege	Minal Sales Agencies, Mumbai

BULK PURCHASES : Tarla Dalal Cookbooks are ideal gifts. If you are interested in buying more than 500 assorted copies of Tarla Dalal Cookbooks at special prices, please contact us at 91-22-4345 2400 or email : sanjay@tarladalal.com

Introduction

Dear Friends,

Home remedies have, since ancient times, retained an important place in the treatment and prevention of illness. Since 2000 years, we have been using herbs from our kitchens, fields and forests to reduce pain and cure illness.

Through the ages India's wide variety of herbs, spices and plants have played a great role in the accumulation and advancement of ancient medical knowledge. **Owing to their easy availability, low cost and absence of side effects, they are becoming increasingly popular once again.** Home remedies have the added advantage by which they help our body mechanisms to *fight disease* unlike modern medicines that can greatly weaken the system in due course of time.

The modern urbanite, from infancy through adulthood to old age is subjected to a continuous chemical bombarding. The use of home remedies can check this unnecessary synthetic drugging which could develop resistance to antibiotics from over use, thereby making them ineffective when we actually need them.

This book comprises of home remedies for 20 ailments with *4 to 6 remedies for each ailment, as every individual reacts in a different way, and therefore, a remedy that may be helpful to one individual may not find be suitable to other.* These remedies have been noted from personal experiences; both mine and those of friends and family and have been verified with the data available in medical literature. **I have worked on 45 recipes using ingredients which are natural and easily available on most kitchen shelves.** Not only are they going to heal but also appeal to your taste buds....

These remedies, however, are not replacements for medical advice from your physician.

Though the remedies recommended are interesting and delicious, the best medicine is preventive medicine. So, eat healthy, exercise and take care of yourself before an illness takes hold.

Tarla Dalal

3

Contents

1. ACIDITY / HEARTBURN

What's Acidity?

Acidity is a form of indigestion in which there is accumulation of acid leading to a burning sensation in the stomach and the digestive tract.

The stomach periodically produces acid to aid digestion. It is when we don't eat at regular intervals or are excessively stressed that the stomach produces more acids which harm our body.

Why does it Happen?

✧ Irregular meals
✧ Oily and spicy foods
✧ Stress
✧ Overeating

Symptoms of Acidity

✧ Burning sensation in the digestive tract
✧ Headache
✧ Sour burps

6

✧ Dizziness due to hypoglycemia (low blood sugar levels)

Remedies
Here are a few kitchen remedies that are sure to ease your discomfort...

➢ **Kokum:** Sherbet made with kokum and perked with jeera is excellent in keeping acidity at bay. Refer to the recipe of *Kokum Sherbet, page 9*.

➢ **Lemon:** Juice of one lemon mixed in half a glass of water and ½ tsp sugar if consumed before meals helps to relieve acidity.

➢ **Vegetable juices:** Juices of vegetables like carrot, cucumber, radish or beetroot help to balance the acid in the stomach due to their alkaline nature. Feel free to add a pinch of salt and pepper to enhance the flavour of these juices.

➢ **Mint:** Fresh mint juice taken every day or fresh mint leaves boiled in a cup of water and sipped slowly after meals also helps to keep the stomach acids at bay.

➢ **Onion (pyaz):** The juice of onions is an excellent remedy for acidity. Have raw onions in salads with your meals or alternatively, you can also try whole wheat or jowar rotis made with onions as done in the recipe of *Jowar Pyaz ki Roti, page 11*.

Foods to be Avoided

◇ Tea and coffee
◇ Pickles, canned and preserved foods
◇ Vinegar
◇ Acidic fruits like orange, sweet lime, strawberry etc.
◇ Confectionery and mithai
◇ Fermented foods like idli, dosa, dhokla, bread, cheese etc.
◇ Toovar (arhar) dal

How can Acidity be Prevented?

1. Regular eating habits and a healthy diet can prevent acidity.
2. Do not remain hungry for a long time. Have plenty of raw foods, salads and juices and avoid spicy or deep fried foods.
3. Eat in a calm and stress-free environment. Avoid irregular and hurried meals.
4. Have your evening meals at least two to three hours before going to bed.
5. Drink plenty of water (at least 6 to 8 glasses per day) and other fluids to maintain the acid balance in the stomach.
6. Avoid smoking and alcohol.

⋏ Kokum Sherbet ⋏

This chilled sherbet is a healthy substitute for carbonated or caffienated drinks and is a great acidity reliever.

Preparation time : 20 minutes.   Cooking time : 15 minutes.   Makes 12 to 15 glasses.

1 cup semi-dried kokum
1 cup sugar
1 tsp roasted cumin (jeera) powder
½ tsp black salt (sanchal)

1. Soak the kokum in 1 cup of water for 2 to 3 hours. Drain and preserve the kokum water.
2. Purée the kokum in a blender using ½ cup of the preserved kokum water, to obtain a smooth purée.
3. Combine the sugar with the remaining kokum water to obtain a 1 string consistency sugar syrup.
4. Cool the sugar syrup. Add the puréed kokum, roasted cumin powder and black salt. Strain and pour into a sterilized air-tight bottle.

5. When serving, add 1 tbsp of this syrup into a tall glass along with 3 to 4 ice-cubes and top with cold water.
6. Stir and serve immediately.

Handy tip: Semi-dried kokums are available at most provision stores. When kokum is in season, use the fresh ones.

⊥ Jowar Pyaz ki Roti ⊥

A combination of jowar and onion that's simply brimming with goodness and is extremely satiating. Serve these hot and remember to chew well as the juice of onion is a boon for acidity.

Preparation time : 5 minutes.   Cooking time : 20 minutes.   Makes 4 rotis.

1 cup jowar flour (white millet flour)
½ cup finely chopped spring onions
1 green chilli, finely chopped
1 tbsp oil
salt to taste

1. Combine all the ingredients in a bowl and knead into a soft dough, using warm water as required.
2. Cover and keep aside for 10 minutes.
3. Divide the dough into 4 equal portions.
4. Pat each portion on a dry surface using your palm into a circle of 125 mm. (5") diameter.

5. Cook on a tava (griddle) over a medium flame till both sides are lightly browned. Serve hot with a vegetable of your choice or fresh cruds.

Handy tip: If you want to roll out these rotis, you can do so between 2 sheets of plastic.

2. ANAEMIA

What's Anaemia?

Anaemia in simple terms is a decrease in the quantity of haemoglobin or in the number of red blood cells (RBC) in the blood. Haemoglobin is made up of *haeme* (iron) and *globin* (protein) which is required for supplying oxygen and nutrients to all parts of our body.

What causes Anaemia?

- Deficiency of iron, vitamin B_{12} or folic acid
- Excessive blood loss or surgery
- Worm infestation in the stomach and intestine
- Pregnancy or lactation due to increased requirements of nutrients (like iron, vitamin B_{12} and folic acid)

How can I know I have Anaemia?

- Weakness
- Fatigue and dizziness
- Loss of appetite and / or constipation

Remedies

Adapting your diet to include foods which contain iron, vitamin B$_{12}$ and folic acid helps to eliminate anaemia. A glance below at the following remedies will help you to do just the same.

➤ If anaemia is caused by a deficiency of folic acid or vitamin B$_{12}$ increase your intake of mushrooms, green leafy vegetables like fenugreek (methi) and other foods like broccoli, milk and wheat germ. Folic acid is a volatile nutrient and is destroyed by heat and light. So, it is wiser to eat fresh fruits and vegetables cooked as little as possible to preserve their goodness.

➤ **Green leafy vegetables:** Green leafy vegetables like spinach (palak), lettuce, celery, fenugreek (methi) etc. are the richest sources of iron, folic acid and vitamin B$_{12}$ and hence should be consumed in abundance. Try to have at least 100 to 125 grams of one leafy vegetable everyday either raw or cooked. You can incorporate these vegetables in the form of Methi Thepla, Spinach Soup, Palak Paneer etc.

➤ **Soyabean:** Soyabean is a valuable source of iron, vitamin B$_{12}$ and protein. A quarter cup of soya everyday in the form of beans or flour is highly effective in combating anaemia. Other forms of soya are milk, tofu (soya paneer), soya nuggets, granules etc. You can mix 100 grams of soya flour with 1 kg. of wheat flour and use the mixture to make chapatis. Refer to the recipes of *Soya Mutter ki Subzi, page 17* and *Soya Upma, page 18*, for delicious soya preparations.

➤ **Black sesame seeds (til):** Black sesame seeds are an extremely rich source of iron. Two tbsp of soaked and puréed mixture of these seeds is beneficial if taken early in the morning. Alternatively, you can also try the recipe of *Almond Til Chikki, page 21*.

➤ **Almonds (badam):** Almonds are a rich source of iron and copper, both of which are important nutrients which together help in the synthesis of haemoglobin. Seven almonds should be soaked in water for about 2 hours and consumed every morning, chewing them properly.

➤ **Other foods:** Foods like dates, jaggery, nachni (ragi) are also very rich sources of iron. Make them a part of your regular meals and say goodbye to anaemia. Have the *Date Honey Banana Shake, page 74*, for a quick and nutritious breakfast or snack.

Foods to be Avoided
✧ Tea and coffee
✧ Refined foods like refined flour, pasta, sugar and polished rice
✧ Ready-to-eat foods like wafers, popcorn etc.
✧ Canned and preserved foods

3 Easy Steps to Combat Anaemia

1. Vitamin C helps in effective absorption of iron in the body. Have plenty of vitamin C rich fruits like oranges, sweet lime, amla etc. along with iron rich foods. A simple way to enhance the intake of vitamin C is to squeeze the juice of lemon on leafy vegetables or have a glass of a citrus fruit juice with each meal to enhance the absorption of iron in the body.
2. Try and replace sugar with jaggery to sweeten foods wherever possible as the latter is a good source of iron.
3. Have whole grains like whole wheat, bajra, buckwheat, brown rice etc. as they are rich sources of iron. Serve iron fortified breakfast cereals especially to children to boost their systems with iron for healthy growth.

⊥ Soya Mutter ki Subzi ⊥

*Soya nuggets are processed from soyabeans to make them more digestible and palatable.
They are a very rich source of protein, vitamin A, vitamin B_{12},
calcium and iron.*

Preparation time : 10 minutes.   Cooking time : 40 minutes.   Serves 2.

½ cup soya nuggets
½ cup green peas, boiled
½ tsp cumin seeds (jeera)
a pinch asafoetida (hing)
1 tsp ginger-green chilli paste
½ tsp garlic paste
1 cup chopped onions
1 cup finely chopped tomatoes
¼ tsp turmeric powder (haldi)
½ tsp chilli powder
½ tsp coriander (dhania) powder
¼ cup fresh curds
2 tsp Bengal gram flour (besan)

2 tbsp milk
½ tsp sugar
1 tbsp oil
salt to taste

1. Soak the soya nuggets in hot salted water for about 20 minutes. Drain and keep aside.
2. Heat the oil in a pan and add the cumin seeds. When they crackle, add the asafoetida, ginger-green chilli paste, garlic paste and onions and sauté till the onions are translucent.
3. Add the tomatoes, turmeric powder, chilli powder and coriander powder and cook on a slow flame for about 5 to 10 minutes.
4. Mix the curds, gram flour, milk and ¾ cup of water and add to the onion-tomato gravy.
5. Add the soya nuggets, green peas, sugar and salt and simmer for 2 more minutes. Serve hot.

⅄ Soya Upma ⅄

Vegetarian diets are deficient in Vitamin B$_{12}$, but soyabean and its by products are an excellent vegetarian source of this vitamin. Soya granules or nuggets provide plenty of protein, energy and calcium too. If you have nuggets instead of granules at home, simply soak and drain them and then chop them finely. Lemon juice contributes vitamin C that aids in the absorption of iron from food. Whip up this nutritive upma that is loaded with vegetables and is also much more nutritious than plain semolina upma.

Preparation time : 20 minutes.   Cooking time : 10 minutes.   Serves 4.

¾ cup soya granules
1 tsp cumin seeds (jeera)
1 tbsp urad dal (split black lentils)
¼ tsp asafoetida (hing)
1 tsp grated ginger
1 to 2 green chillies, slit
½ cup chopped onions
½ cup grated carrots
½ cup chopped cabbage
juice of ½ lemon

1 tbsp oil
salt to taste

For the garnish
2 tbsp chopped coriander
4 lemon wedges

1. Soak the soya granules in hot water for approx. 15 minutes. Drain, squeeze out all the water and keep aside. Discard the water.
2. Heat the oil in a pan and add the cumin seeds. When they crackle, add the urad dal and sauté till the dal turns light brown.
3. Add the asafoetida, ginger, green chillies and onions.
4. Sauté the onions till they are translucent. Add the carrots and cabbage and sauté for another 4 to 5 minutes.
5. Add the soya granules and mix well.
6. Season with salt and mix again.
   Serve hot garnished with the chopped coriander and lemon wedges.

⚲ Almond Til Chikki ⚲

This is a healthy sweet treat as both black sesame seeds and almonds are rich in iron.

Preparation time : 10 minutes.   Cooking time : 10 minutes.   Makes 10 pieces.

½ cup black sesame seeds (til)
½ cup thinly sliced almonds (badam)
⅓ cup grated jaggery (gur)
1 tsp ghee

Other ingredients
½ tsp ghee for greasing

1. Roast the sesame seeds for a few minutes over a medium flame till they are light golden in colour. Cool and keep aside. Repeat with the almonds.
2. Grease the back of a flat thali or a stone surface with a little ghee and keep aside.
3. Heat the ghee in a pan and add the jaggery to it.
4. Simmer over a slow flame till the jaggery melts and caramelizes and forms a hard ball when you add a drop in cold water. Remove from the flame.

5. Add the roasted sesame seeds and almonds and mix thoroughly with the melted jaggery. You may need to put off the flame during this process.
6. When the mixture is ready, pour the entire mixture over the greased thali or a smooth stone surface. Roll the chikki out into thin sheets using a greased rolling pin.
7. When cool, cut into square pieces. Store in an air-tight container.

3. ANOREXIA

What's Anorexia?
Anorexia is loss of appetite i.e. lack of interest in eating. This can cause weight loss and weakness.

What causes Anorexia?
- ✦ Emotional stress or depression
- ✦ Medication
- ✦ Sickness
- ✦ Inactive lifestyle

Remedies
These natural remedies are sure to help perk up your appetite.

- ➤ **Mint (phudina):** 1 to 2 tbsp of mint juice daily in the morning helps to whet your appetite.

- **Apple:** The old saying "An apple a day, keeps the doctor away" stays true for anorexic individuals as apples aid in digestion and also boost your appetite.

- **Ajwain (carom seeds):** Swallowing 1 tsp of ajwain with or without water, 3 to 4 times a day is another remedy to enhance your appetite.

- **Asafoetida (hing):** Two pinches of asafoetida mixed in 2 tsp of ghee when taken before meals also helps to overcome anorexia.

- **Pineapple:** Having a few pieces of pineapple sprinkled with salt and black pepper helps to restore lost appetite, especially for kids.

- **Lemon:** Equal quantities of lemon and ginger juice should be consumed every day before meals to decrease anorexia. Alternatively, *Appetizing Drink, page 26*, is also a good remedy to perk up your appetite.

Foods to be Avoided
- ✧ Tea and coffee
- ✧ Aerated drinks
- ✧ Refined foods like refined flour, pasta, sugar and polished rice
- ✧ Ready-to-eat foods like wafers, popcorn etc.

Practical Tips for Enhancing Appetite

1. Eat in a relaxed and calm environment and make it a pleasurable experience and not a "task" that has to be completed.
2. Have frequent and small snacks that are healthy and are high in protein and calories. Try a filling shake or a glass of fruit juice like *Fruit Cocktail, page 27,* if you don't feel like eating much.
3. Have variety in terms of colour and texture of food to be served. Present foods in a child-like fun way. Make sandwiches into interesting shapes or decorate fruits, breads and vegetables with interesting toppings.
4. Avoid drinking liquids at meal times as they can give a feeling of fullness causing you to eat less.
5. Have a walk before meals if possible. Fresh air often helps to perk up our appetite, as does a little activity.

⚑ Appetizing Drink ⚑

*Sip this about ½ an hour before your meals and I assure you will develop
a healthy appetite.*

Preparation time : 1 to 2 minutes.　Cooking time : 10 minutes.　Makes 1 cup.

¼ tsp asafoetida (hing)
¼ tsp crushed peppercorns
1½ tsp lemon juice
¼ tsp salt

1. Combine the asafoetida, crushed peppercorns and salt with 1 cup of water and simmer for about 8 to 10 minutes.
2. Add the lemon juice and strain.
   Serve immediately.

⅄ **Fruit Cocktail** ⅄

Have this filling fruit cocktail in case you are on the run or are not really hungry. The natural fruit sugar will keep you going for hours. The fruits will also provide all the essential vitamins, minerals and fibre you require.

Preparation time : 25 minutes.   No cooking.   Serves 2.

1½ cups chopped apple
1 cup black grapes
1 cup peeled and chopped pineapple
½ cup orange juice
1 tbsp glucose powder
salt and pepper to taste
crushed ice

1. Combine all the fruits in a blender and purée.
2. Just before serving, add the glucose, salt, pepper and crushed ice and mix well. Serve immediately in tall glasses.

4. CALCIUM DEFICIENCY

All about Calcium Deficiency

Calcium is required for the growth and strengthening of bones and teeth. Calcium deficiency is one of the most common problems that begins at childhood and resurfaces during pregnancy or old age.

Causes of Calcium Deficiency

- ✧ Inadequate intake of calcium rich foods
- ✧ Defective absorption of nutrients in the stomach and intestine
- ✧ Other conditions like vitamin D deficiency, liver disease etc.

Symptoms of Calcium Deficiency

- ✧ Brittle bones
- ✧ Joint pains
- ✧ Yellowing of teeth
- ✧ In extreme cases, rickets (soft bones) in children and osteoporosis (brittle bones) in adults

Remedies

Make these ingredients a part of your daily diet to chase away calcium deficiency.

➤ **Dairy products:** Consumption of calcium rich dairy products like milk, curds, paneer and buttermilk is one of the best ways to rebuild your calcium reserves.

➤ **Green leafy vegetables:** Green leafy vegetables like spinach (palak), lettuce, celery (ajwain ka patta), fenugreek (methi) etc. are also good sources of calcium and hence should be consumed in abundance. *Sai Bhaji, page 31*, a mixture of 3 green leafy vegetables is a very simple way of incorporating them in our diet.

➤ **Soyabean:** Soyabean and its products like soya flour, soya milk, tofu etc. are valuable sources of calcium and protein. A quarter to half cup of soyabeans in any form is beneficial for those with calcium deficiency. A vegetable made with soyabeans in a gravy or chapatis made with soya flour are the most acceptable dishes for both children and adults. *Soya Mutter ki Subzi, page 17* and *Soya Upma, page 18*, are perfect examples of including soya in our daily meal.

➤ **Ragi (nachni):** Ragi, a popular Maharashtrian cereal, is another rich source of calcium. A quarter cup of ragi, either whole or in the form of flour consumed daily helps to cure calcium deficiency. Try the calcium rich *Nachni Pancakes, page 33*, to boost your calcium intake.

➤ **Sesame seeds (til):** Having 1 to 2 tsp of sesame seeds everyday is an effective way to keep calcium deficiency at bay. Try consuming them in salads or in the form of chikki as in the recipe of *Almond Til Chikki, page 21*.

Foods to be Avoided

✧ Deep fried foods
✧ Refined foods like refined flour, pasta, sugar and polished rice

Pointers for Increasing Calcium Intake

1. Include at least one source of calcium in every meal.
2. Have at least 100 to 125 grams of one leafy vegetable everyday, either cooked or uncooked.
3. Consume 2 to 3 glasses of milk in any form (like curds, paneer etc.) to supplement calcium in your diet. Overweight people can use low calorie milk products.
4. Restrict the consumption of fat, as excessive fat hinders the absorption of calcium in the body.
5. Have a sunbath every morning, as the early morning sunlight is good for the production of vitamin D which in turn helps in the synthesis of calcium in our body.

▲ Sai Bhaji ▲

This traditional Sindhi recipe is a good combination of leafy vegetables with dal which provides plenty of calcium, protein, iron and vitamin A. Relish it with steamed rice or any kind of roti.

Preparation time : 10 minutes.   Cooking time : 25 minutes.   Serves 4.

3 tbsp chana dal (split Bengal gram)
3 cups chopped spinach (palak)
¾ cup chopped khatta bhaji (khatta palak)
¾ cup chopped chawli (cow pea) leaves
½ tsp cumin seeds (jeera)
½ cup chopped onions
1 cup chopped potatoes
½ cup chopped brinjals (baingan)
2 tsp ginger-garlic paste
1 tsp chilli powder
2 tsp coriander (dhania) powder
a pinch turmeric powder (haldi)
1 tbsp oil

salt to taste

1. Combine the chana dal with 1 cup of water and pressure cook for 1 whistle. Drain the excess water and keep aside.
2. Heat the oil in a pressure cooker and add the cumin seeds.
3. When the seeds crackle, add the onions, potatoes, brinjals and ginger-garlic paste and sauté for 5 to 7 minutes.
4. Add the chilli powder, coriander powder, turmeric powder and salt and sauté for 2 to 3 minutes.
5. Add the spinach, khatta bhaji, chawli leaves and the cooked chana dal and pressure cook for 2 whistles.
6. Allow it to cool and whisk the mixture well.
   Serve hot.

Handy tip : Khatta bhaji is available at most vegetable vendors. It looks like a smaller version of spinach leaves and the leaves are slightly sour in taste.

⋏ Nachni Pancakes ⋏

Wholesome, quick and easy dosas made with ragi. Ragi is a cereal which is not very commonly consumed by many of us. But you would be surprised to know that it is one of the greatest sources of calcium. So here's a calcium boost just for you.

Preparation time : 15 minutes.   Cooking time : 20 minutes.   Makes 6 pancakes.

1 cup ragi (nachni) flour
1 tbsp soya flour (optional)
1 tsp sesame seeds (til)
½ cup finely chopped onions
2 green chillies, finely chopped
1 tsp grated ginger
½ cup chopped coriander
salt to taste
oil for cooking

1. In a bowl, combine the ragi flour, soya flour, sesame seeds, onions, green chillies, ginger, coriander and salt and mix well.

2. Heat a non-stick pan and grease it with a little oil.
3. Spread an even layer of the batter to make a 125 mm. (5") round.
4. Cook on both sides till golden brown, using a little oil.
5. Repeat with the rest of the batter to make 5 more pancakes.
   Serve hot with a chutney of your choice.

5. COMMON COLD AND COUGH

What's a Common Cold and Cough?

A common cold is called so because it's the commonest of all ailments and affects most of us more frequently than any other ailment.

Throat irritation and blockage of the nasal passage usually accompanies a cold. It may also be accompanied by a cough which is the secretion of mucus due to infection of the lungs.

What causes Cold and Cough?

There is no exact reason for the cold and cough. Its causes can vary from an allergy, influenza, sinusitis or a viral infection. However the most common reasons are:

- ✧ Low immunity
- ✧ Exposure to cold or dust
- ✧ Other irritating inhalations
- ✧ Allergies

Symptoms of Cold and Cough

- ✧ Runny nose

- ❖ Secretion of mucus
- ❖ Throat irritation

Remedies

Here are some soothing natural remedies that will help keep you smiling through the cold.

➤ **Vitamin C rich fruits:** Vitamin C rich fruits such as oranges, sweet limes, strawberries, lemons etc. are extremely effective in treating and keeping cold and cough away. The high amount of vitamin C in these fruits increases the body's resistance to virus and decreases the duration of the illness. An easy way to enhance your intake of vitamin C is to squeeze a lemon in a glass of warm water, sweeten it with a tsp of honey and drink it twice daily for at least 3 days.

➤ **Ginger (adrak):** Cut about 10 grams of ginger into small pieces and boil in a cup of water. Strain, add a tsp of sugar and drink it while hot. Alternatively, Ginger Tea or *Spicy Masala Tea, page 81* is also an effective remedy against cold.

➤ **Garlic (lehsun):** Garlic is a real immunity booster. Finely chop 2 to 3 cloves of garlic and swallow it like any other medicine. It can also be used raw into salad dressings. Crushing a clove of garlic into soups, stews etc. is also effective and greatly enhances their flavour. See the recipe of *Garlic Vegetable Soup, page 101.*

➤ **Turmeric powder (haldi):** Turmeric is most effective in curing throat irritation during colds. Fresh turmeric powder and ajwain (carom seeds) mixed in a glass of warm milk taken once or twice a day is the most useful curative measure. See the recipe of *Ajwain and Turmeric Milk, page 124.*

Foods to be Avoided

✧ Cold beverages, aerated drinks and ice-creams
✧ Deep fried foods
✧ Confectionery and mithai

Easy Pointers to Fight Cold and Cough

1. Consume plenty of fresh fruits and vegetables as they abound in nutrients which strengthen the immune system. Try not to cook the vegetables for a long period as it results in loss of volatile nutrients like vitamins B and C.
2. Drink plenty of fluids (water, vegetable soups and fruit juices) as they help to replenish the fluids lost during the illness.
3. Eat hot and spicy foods. Eating these foods will make your nose run and the mucus will begin to clear. Spicy foods work just like a natural decongestant without any side effects. Try out the *Cold Reliever, page 39*, and the spicy Chinese delicacy, *Mein Chow Soup, page 41.*

4. Avoid smoking as it aggravates the throat and interferes with the infection-fighting activity of the cells.
5. Take rest as it gives your body a better chance to fight the virus.
6. Stay away from a dusty environment as that can aggravate the situation.

⅄ **Cold Reliever** ⅄

A caffeine free tea made with only natural herbs to soothe your throat and help expel mucus. It is also called kasai or kadha.

Preparation time: 5 minutes.   Cooking time : 5 minutes.   Makes 1 cup.

1½ tbsp of spice powder (recipe below)
1½ tsp misri (khadi sakhar)
2 tbsp milk

For the spice powder
¼ cup coriander (dhania) seeds
1½ tbsp cumin seeds (jeera)
1½ tbsp fennel seeds (saunf)
¼ tsp fenugreek (methi) seeds

For the spice powder
1. Dry roast all the ingredients on a tava (griddle) and grind to a coarse powder.
2. Cool and store in an air-tight container. Use as required.

How to proceed
1. Boil 1 cup of water and add the spice powder and misri to it.
2. Simmer for about 3 to 4 minutes and then add the milk.
3. Bring to a boil, strain and serve.
4. Sip while it is hot for best results.

⊿ Mein Chow Soup ⊿

Thick, hot and spicy, flavoured with mint and coriander is all I can say about this soup. It is sure to free you from nose blocks and help to overcome the cold.

Preparation time : 15 minutes.   Cooking time : 10 minutes.   Serves 4.

4½ cups clear vegetable stock or water
2 tbsp finely chopped tomatoes
2 tbsp finely chopped capsicum
2 tbsp finely chopped cauliflower
2 tbsp finely chopped carrots
2 tbsp finely chopped cabbage
1 tbsp finely chopped fresh mint leaves
1 tbsp chopped coriander
2 tsp finely chopped garlic
2 tsp finely chopped ginger
3 tsp soya sauce
2 tbsp cornflour mixed in ½ cup of water
a pinch Ajinomoto powder (optional)

1 tbsp oil
salt and pepper to taste

For the topping
chilli oil
chopped coriander

For serving
soya sauce

1. Heat the oil in a wok over a high flame. Add the garlic, ginger, vegetables and stir-fry for 2 to 3 minutes over a high flame.
2. Add the stock, mint, coriander, soya sauce, Ajinomoto, salt and pepper.
3. Add the cornflour paste to the soup and boil for 1 minute. Top with the chilli oil and coriander.
   Serve hot with soya sauce.

Handy tip: To make clear vegetable stock quickly, just add roughly cut carrots, onions and celery to a vesselful of water and boil for about 15 minutes. Then strain and discard the vegetables. The leftover liquid is clear vegetable stock.

6. CONSTIPATION

What's Constipation?
Constipation is a condition of the bowels in which evacuation is difficult and infrequent.

What causes Constipation?
- ❖ Insufficient fibre in the diet
- ❖ Weakness of abdominal muscles due to lack of physical activity
- ❖ Improper chewing of food
- ❖ Over consumption of alcohol or caffeineated beverages
- ❖ Emotional stress

Remedies
Fibre, fibre, fibre is the magic remedy to this common malady...

➤ **Dates (khajur):** Have 4 to 5 dates every day early in the morning.

➤ **Fibre rich fruits:** The high fibre content in these fruits adds bulk to our diet thus regulating bowel movements and preventing constipation. Have at least 1 to 2 fibre rich fruits like orange, sweet lime, pineapple, grapes, guava etc. at bedtime to overcome constipation. You can also try the recipe of an unstrained juice like *Beach Tropicana, page 46.*

➤ **Papaya:** Papaya is another effective laxative. Have a cup of chopped papaya with breakfast every day to stimulate bowel movements.

➤ **Lemon water:** Half a lime squeezed in a glass of hot water with ½ tsp of salt is a very effective remedy for constipation. Have it early in the morning even before your mandatory cuppa tea or coffee to regularize the bowel movements.

➤ **Fennel seeds (saunf):** Fennel seeds are well known for their digestive properties. A decoction made by boiling fennel seeds in water is a great laxative.

Foods to be Avoided
◆ Tea and coffee
◆ Aerated drinks
◆ Refined foods like refined flour, pasta, sugar and polished rice
◆ Deep fried foods

◇ Confectionery and mithai
◇ Fast foods like pizzas, burgers etc.

Tips to Avoid and Overcome Constipation

Listed below are a few simple tips that are sure to ease your discomfort.

1. Eat a high fibre breakfast as fibre stimulates bowel movements.
2. Drink plenty of fluids (at least 6 to 8 glasses every day) as this softens the stools making them easier to pass.
3. Consume plenty of fruits and vegetables (with their skin on), whole grains such as whole wheat, oats, to the stools and help in bowel movements. One flavourful way of adding these fruits and veggies to our diet is *Carrot and Date Salad, page 47.*
4. Add high fibre foods like wheat bran or rice bran in your daily meals. An easy way to incorporate fibre in your diet is to add 1 to 2 tbsp of bran to wheat flour while kneading the chapati dough.
5. Encourage daily exercise such as walking as this helps in bowel movements.
6. Maintain a regular morning routine which allows time for bowels to move prior to starting your day.

⚤ Beach Tropicana ⚤

An eye catching fibre rich cocktail whipped up with nature's harvest (fruits).
I have avoided straining this juice to retain the fibre which helps to overcome
constipation.

Preparation time: 10 minutes.   No cooking.   Serves 2.

1 cup peeled and chopped papaya
1 cup peeled and chopped fresh pineapple
1 banana, peeled and sliced
1 tbsp sugar (optional)
¾ cup crushed ice

Blend all the ingredients in a liquidiser till smooth and serve immediately.

⚴ Carrot and Date Salad ⚴

This recipe packs an irresistible combination of carrot and dates with a lemon dressing.
Try this salad as a part of your meal if you are bored of eating only raw veggies or mashed
dates as mentioned above. You can skip the almonds if you are weight conscious.

Preparation time : 15 minutes.   No cooking.   Serves 4.

2 cups grated carrots
2 cups torn lettuce
½ cup chopped dates (khajur)
2 tbsp chopped toasted almonds (optional)

To be mixed into a dressing
2 tsp lemon juice
2 tsp olive oil
½ tsp freshly crushed peppercorns
salt to taste

1. Immerse the lettuce in ice-cold water for 10 minutes. Drain thoroughly.
2. Spread the carrots in the middle of the lettuce leaves and chill.

3. Sprinkle the dates and almonds over the carrots.
4. Just before serving, toss the dressing into the salad. Serve immediately.

7. DEFECTIVE VISION

What is Defective Vision?

Defective vision refers to the inability to see objects clearly. This can be inability to see far off objects (short sightedness) or inability to see close by objects (long sightedness). In extreme cases, night blindness (inability to see at night) occurs.

Causes of Defective Vision

❖ Lack of nutrients like vitamin A, vitamin E, protein etc.
❖ Excessive strain on the eyes.

Symptoms of Defective Vision

❖ Watery eyes
❖ Heaviness of the eyes
❖ Headache

Remedies

Here are some important nutrients which will help improve your eyesight.

➤ **Green leafy vegetables:** Leafy vegetables are a storehouse of vitamins A and E, the two nutrients which help us to maintain healthy eyesight. They also abound in iron which is an essential component of blood. Insufficient iron leads to decreased supply of blood to the eyes thus making the vision defective. Feasting on leafy vegetables will help you acquire better eyesight. If you do not enjoy eating raw vegetables, try disguising them in soups, salads, rotis etc. See *Vision Soup, page 52*, for one such variation.

➤ **Whole grains and cereals:** These are also rich sources of vitamin E. Include cereals like wheat, jowar, wheat bran, rice bran etc. as a part of your daily meal. Refined and processed cereals like maida and semolina have very minimal vitamin E as much of it is in the outer covering of grains.

➤ **Vitamin C rich fruits and vegetables:** Vitamin C helps to protect the lens of the eyes. Fruits like orange, sweet lime, guava, papaya, amla etc. and vegetables like broccoli, capsicum, cabbage and all green leafy vegetables are good sources of vitamin C.

➤ **Dals, sprouts and dairy products:** Protein rich foods like dals, sprouts and dairy products are of utmost importance for the formation of a protective chemical in the eyes which is extremely essential for good vision. Include these in your daily cooking and enhance your vision.

Foods to be Avoided

❖ Tea and coffee
❖ Aerated drinks
❖ Refined foods like maida, pasta, sugar and polished rice
❖ Canned and preserved foods
❖ Fast foods like pizzas, burgers etc.
❖ Ready-to-eat foods like wafers, popcorn etc.

Tips to Improve Vision

1. It is best to have raw fruits and vegetables. If you do cook them, try not to overcook as this leads to loss of volatile nutrients like vitamins C and B complex. Try the recipe of *Carrot-n-Celery Sandwich, page 54.*
2. Have at least two glasses of milk every day to make up for your protein requirement.
3. Include sprouts as a part of any one meal of the day. Sprouts abound in protein, iron and vitamin C and are easier to digest than dals.
4. To enhance the absorption of iron, squeeze a little vitamin C rich lemon juice in your daily cooking or have fresh lime juice after meals.

⋏ Vision Soup ⋏

Richness in taste and nutrients like vitamin A, vitamin E vitamin C and iron is what makes this soup a marvellous recipe for healthy vision.

Preparation time : 15 minutes.   Cooking time : 10 minutes.   Serves 4.

1 cup chopped spinach (palak)
½ cup chopped onions
3 tbsp chopped carrots
4 tsp cornflour
2¼ cups milk
1 tbsp butter
salt and pepper to taste

For the topping
wheat germ (2 tbsp approx.)

1. Heat the butter in a pan and sauté the onions for 1 minute. Add the carrots and ¾ cup of water and cool for at least 5 minutes.
2. Add the spinach and sauté again for 1 minute.

3. Mix the cornflour, milk and 1½ cups of water, add to the spinach mixture and simmer for a few minutes. Cool completely.
4. Blend in a liquidiser for a few seconds. Do not strain.
5. Add salt and pepper and bring to a boil. Top with wheat germ and serve hot.

⋏ Carrot-n-Celery Sandwich ⋏

A magic formula for better vision due to the use of 4 multi-nutrient ingredients viz.
tomato, cheese, celery and lettuce. These are perfect to tempt anyone at
snack time and make a great packed lunch as well.

Preparation time : 5 minutes.   No cooking.   Makes 4 sandwiches.

8 whole wheat bread slices
1 large tomato, thinly sliced
4 lettuce leaves
salt and freshly ground pepper to taste

To be mixed into a filling mixture
¾ cup grated carrots
2 tbsp finely chopped celery
1 clove garlic, grated
¼ cup eggless mayonnaise
½ cup cheese spread
½ tsp freshly ground pepper

54

1. Apply a generous layer of the filling mixture on 4 bread slices.
2. Place a large lettuce leaf on top and then the sliced tomatoes.
3. Sprinkle salt and freshly ground pepper.
4. Sandwich each one with the remaining 4 slices of bread.
5. Cut each sandwich diagonally into 2 and serve immediately.

Handy tip: Eggless mayonnaise is readily available at most grocery stores.

8. DIABETES

What's Diabetes?

Diabetes is a condition characterized by high blood sugar (glucose) levels due to a lack or insufficient production of a hormone called insulin in the body. Insulin is responsible for decreasing the blood sugar levels and aids in producing energy for the cells. Without enough insulin, glucose obtained from the food builds up in the blood stream leading to a hike in blood sugar levels above than the normal limits. This causes many health complications.

It is a lifelong condition that can be managed with careful diet control and proper medication (either oral medication or insulin) under your physician's and dietitian's supervision.

What Commonly causes Diabetes?

- ✧ Genetics (heredity)
- ✧ Obesity
- ✧ Irregular and unhealthy eating habits
- ✧ Stress

Remedies

For diabetics, what they eat and when they eat is extremely important. So some modifications in eating habits are very helpful for every individual with diabetes. Here are some delicious ways to make some not-so-palatable foods a part of your lifestyle.

➤ **Karela (bitter gourd):** The juice of karela with seeds or the cooked vegetable is beneficial for diabetics. This helps to reduce sugar levels in the blood as well as in the urine. If you choose to have this drink, it is advisable to do so on an empty stomach or before meals. Try the recipe of *Karela Theplas, page 60,* for an interesting variation.

➤ **Soyabean:** Soyabean in any form like whole beans, soya flour, soya milk have been proved to control the blood sugar levels in diabetics. They are also effective in preventing neurological complications like numbness of feet and shivering of hands that commonly occur among diabetics.

➤ **Black jamun:** The fruit black jamun is said to be a boon for diabetics. This fruit is delicious and can be taken in adequate quantities when in season. An enzyme called jamboline present in this fruit helps to control blood sugar levels. Jamun juice spiked with black salt (sanchal) tastes delicious too and is also a good way of including this fruit in your diet. Dried powder of the leaves of this plant is also very effective in lowering blood sugar levels. One tsp of equal quantities of jamun powder and amla

57

powder has proven to be very useful too.

➤ **Fenugreek (methi):** Both methi seeds and leaves are effective in controlling diabetes. One tsp of methi seeds soaked in water overnight should be consumed with milk the first thing every morning. If you are amongst those who are very fussy about eating methi, try disguising it in your daily meals in the form of rotis, parathas or subzis.

➤ **Chana dal (split Bengal gram):** Research shows that chana dal helps in the utilization of blood sugar effectively thus causing a slow rise in blood sugar levels. Have steamed chana dal and besan based dishes like dhoklas, among others to add this food to your diet.

Foods to be Avoided
✧ Sweeteners like sugar, honey and jaggery
✧ Confectionery and mithai
✧ Refined foods like refined flour, pasta, sugar and polished rice
✧ Deep fried foods
✧ Dried fruits and nuts
✧ Creamy salad dressings
✧ Fruit juices
✧ Aerated drinks

◇ Full fat dairy products
◇ Pickles, canned and preserved foods

Ways to Maintain Blood Sugar Levels

1. Consume plenty of fibre rich foods such as whole cereals, pulses, raw vegetables and fruits as they help to maintain the blood sugar levels. In cereals, whole wheat is better than rice because it contains an enzyme called Ascarbose, which allows carbohydrates to be absorbed slowly. Thus, the blood sugar does not rise rapidly.

2. Have only one source of protein like dal, milk or curds in each meal. If you are used to having thick dal, try to dilute it, as that will cut down on the protein content drastically. Even the buttermilk you consume should be diluted with water to reduce the intake of concentrated protein and fat in your diet.

3. Restrict the consumption of fat to 3 tsp per day.

4. Bake, roast, steam or sauté instead of shallow frying and deep frying. It is also wiser to replace full fat dairy products with their low fat counterparts. Low fat milk has all the goodness of whole milk except the fat which is the culprit for many ailments.

5. Try to eat in a calm atmosphere as stress or anxiety can impair the production of insulin.

6. Walk for 15 to 20 minutes after every meal as exercise utilizes the sugar present in blood and help the insulin to work better.

⊥ Karela Theplas ⊥

The first thing we all can think about karelas is its bitterness. But karela is extremely beneficial for diabetics and one can enjoy it more if you acquire the taste for it. This innovative recipe makes use of the peels of the karela which we usually throw away. Wash and chop the peels into small pieces before adding it to the dough.

Preparation time : 5 minutes.   Cooking time : 15 minutes.   Makes 10 theplas.

1 cup whole wheat flour (gehun ka atta)
¼ cup bajra flour (black millet flour)
½ cup finely chopped karela peels (bitter gourd)
½ tsp grated garlic
½ tsp turmeric powder (haldi)
1 tsp chilli powder
1 tsp coriander (dhania) powder
1 tbsp chopped coriander
salt to taste

Other ingredients
2 tsp oil to brush the theplas

1. Combine all the ingredients and knead into a firm dough using enough water and knead well.
2. Divide the dough into 10 equal parts and roll each portion into a circle of approx. 125 mm. (5") diameter.
3. Cook each one on a non-stick pan till both sides are golden brown.
4. Brush each thepla with a little oil and serve hot.

⋏ Carrot Methi Subzi ⋏

This is a great combination of textures and fragrant, spicy flavours that has the added advantage of being quick to make. Being enriched with vitamin A, iron and fibre, it is nutritious. Avoid peeling the carrots as the peel is rich in fibre. Simply scrub the carrots under running water to remove dirt.

Preparation time : 10 minutes.   Cooking time : 15 minutes.   Serves 4.

2 cups carrots, cut into cubes
2 cups chopped fenugreek (methi) leaves
½ tsp cumin seeds (jeera)
½ cup finely chopped onions
3 to 4 green chillies, finely chopped
1 large clove garlic, finely chopped
12 mm. (½") piece ginger, finely chopped
¼ tsp turmeric powder (haldi)
2 tsp coriander (dhania) powder
2 tsp oil
salt to taste

1. Heat the oil in a non-stick pan and add the cumin seeds.
2. When they crackle, add the onions, green chillies, garlic and ginger and sauté for 2 minutes.
3. Add the fenugreek leaves and sauté for another 2 minutes.
4. Add the carrots, turmeric powder, coriander powder, salt and 1 cup of water and stir.
5. Cover and cook over a slow flame till all the moisture has evaporated and the carrots are tender.

   Serve hot with phulkas.

9. DIARRHOEA

What is Diarrhoea?

Diarrhoea is referred to as frequent passage of watery stools which leads to the depletion of fluids and salts (sodium and potassium) that are responsible for maintaining the fluid balance in our body.

What causes Diarrhoea?

- ✧ Food poisoning
- ✧ Allergy to certain foods
- ✧ Over eating
- ✧ Overuse of laxatives

Remedies

➤ **Salt and sugar:** The best way to replenish the lost fluids is to mix a tsp each of salt and sugar in a cup of water and sip it as many times as you can.

➤ **Fenugreek (methi) seeds:** One tsp of fenugreek seeds should be swallowed (without chewing) with a cup of curds, buttermilk or water for immediate relief.

> **Mint (phudina):** One tsp of mint leaves mixed with a tsp each of lime juice and honey should be given thrice daily for excellent results. You can also try the recipe of *Lemon Phudina Pani, page 67.*

> **Apples:** A cooked or a baked apple taken everyday is a good medicine for diarrhoea because it contains fibre. Fibre binds the stool together in diahrroea and helps control it.

> **Garlic (lehsun):** Garlic is yet another natural remedy that fights diarrhoea and helps to kill parasites. It is a powerful and effective antibiotic and aids digestion too.

Foods to be Avoided
✧ Spicy and oily foods
✧ Confectionery, mithai and chocolates
✧ Fermented foods like dhokla, bread, idlis, dosas, cheese etc.
✧ Uncooked fruits and vegetables

Healthy Diet during Diarrhoea
1. Consume small and light meals frequently instead of 3 big meals a day to replenish the lost nutrients.
2. Have plenty of fluids like lemon juice, fruit juices, vegetable soups (of carrot, spinach

etc.), watery dals (of barley, moong dal etc.), lassi, coconut water etc. to make up for the loss of fluids. *Rice Porridge, page 68,* is also an excellent alternative to restore the fluid levels.

3. Have fruits like banana and apple as they are rich in potassium which helps to maintain the fluid balance in our body.
4. Try to restrict the consumption of milk and other dairy products in the beginning, as these are difficult to digest. If you must eat, curds is the best choice of all dairy products to digest.

Tips to Avoid Diarrhoea

1. Always wash your hands twice with soap before eating anything and dry your hands with a clean towel as wet hands carry a significant risk of infection.
2. Eat only fresh foods that have been well cooked. Raw foods like salads can irritate your system.
3. Avoid local drinking water in places where there is a high risk. Have packaged water instead.
4. Avoid consuming foods from food stalls on the street, though they may seem exciting, because they are unhygienic.
5. Avoid consuming chilled drinks. This does not cause infection but may lead to stomach cramps.

⅄ Lemon Phudina Pani ⅄

This combination of lemon and mint sweetened with honey and perked with cumin seeds if consumed thrice a day helps to curtail diarrhoea almost immediately.

Preparation time : 10 minutes.   No cooking.   Makes 2 cups.

1 cup finely chopped mint (phudina) leaves
1 tbsp lemon juice
2 tbsp honey
½ tsp salt
¼ tsp roasted cumin seeds (jeera)
2 cups water

1. Mix all the ingredients and liquidise in a blender.
2. Chill for an hour so that the flavours blend well.

▲ Rice Porridge ▲

Easy to digest and full of nutrients, this porridge is sure to replenish in you the lost fluid and salt balance.

Preparation time : 10 minutes.   Cooking time : 20 minutes.   Makes 2½ cups.

¼ cup rice
½ tsp cumin seeds (jeera)
½ tsp ghee
salt to taste

1. Wash the rice and drain the water.
2. Heat the ghee in a pressure cooker and add the cumin seeds.
3. When the cumin seeds crackle, add the rice and salt along with 3 to 4 cups of water and pressure cook for 4 to 6 whistles.
4. Whisk the mixture well and simmer uncovered for 5 to 7 minutes till the desired consistency is obtained.
   Serve hot.

10. FATIGUE

What is Fatigue?

Fatigue is defined as a feeling of tiredness due to exertion that can be both mental and physical. Fatigue is not just the feeling of exhaustion one feels after doing something strenuous, but it is when one is tired all the time and cannot seem to recover.

What causes Fatigue?

Fatigue does not always seem to have an obvious cause, but the most common reasons are:

◇ Stress or excessive physical activity.
◇ A complete lack of activity can also lead to fatigue, which can also be a by-product of boredom and depression.
◇ Certain medical conditions like low blood sugar levels, anaemia or damage to liver, heart or kidney can also cause fatigue.
◇ Deficiency of certain vitamins and minerals like iron, calcium and vitamin D can also be a cause for fatigue.

Remedies

The following foods are sure to de-stress you and chase all the fatigue away.

➤ **Fruits and vegetables:** Have plenty of fruits and vegetables as they provide all the necessary vitamins and minerals to keep us going. Vitamins and minerals boost our bodies with positive energy and keep us feeling light, yet full.

➤ **Protein rich foods:** Consume protein rich foods like dairy products, dals, pulses and cereals to strengthen the muscles. Having ¼ cup of sprouts every morning helps to reduce the fatigue in the latter part of the day. Try my recipe of *Bean Sprouts Salad, page 72*.

➤ **Dates (khajur):** Two or three dates boiled in milk for 8 to 10 minutes helps to eliminate fatigue.

➤ **Banana:** Have two ripe bananas everyday (either as a snack or along with your meals) as they contain plenty of pick-me- up nutrients. *Date Honey Banana Shake, page 74*, is a delicious remedy to overcome fatigue.

➤ **Almonds (badam):** A drink made with a mixture of almonds, figs and warm milk helps to relieve fatigue instantly.

Foods to be Avoided

✧ Tea and coffee
✧ Deep fried foods
✧ Refined foods like maida, pasta, sugar and polished rice
✧ Canned and preserved foods
✧ Fast foods like pizzas, burgers etc.

Handy Hints to Avoid and Overcome Fatigue

1. Indulge in any activity you enjoy. Listen to music, go for a walk or cook as it will keep the mind and body fresh and alert.
2. Never miss your breakfast. It provides you the needed energy and keeps you going throughout the day.
3. Listen to your hunger pangs. Do not starve. Have a small snack in between meals, even if it's a piece of fruit or toast, to keep you going till the next meal. Try *Magaz, page 75,* for one of the small meals of the day.
4. Consume protein rich foods more frequently. For example, sprouts, dals and dairy products in any form.
5. Drink plenty of water.
6. Include plenty of fruits in your daily diet as they contain fructose, a fruit sugar, which acts as an instant pick me up.

⋏ Bean Sprouts Salad ⋏

Sprouts are full of vitamins and easy to digest. This easy to make salad which is healthy, colourful and crunchy can be enjoyed at any time of the day.

Preparation time : 15 minutes.   No cooking.   Serves 4.

1½ cups bean sprouts (washed and drained)
1½ cups cucumber, peeled and cut into thin strips
½ cup diced spring onions

For the garnish
3 tbsp roasted peanuts

To be mixed into a dressing
2 tbsp lemon juice
1 tbsp castor sugar
2 tbsp olive oil
½ tsp mustard (rai) powder
salt and pepper to taste

For the dressing
1. Shake the ingredients thoroughly in a closed bottle.
2. Chill and use as required.

How to proceed
1. Combine the bean sprouts, cucumber and spring onions in a bowl and chill.
2. Just before serving, add the dressing as required and toss.
   Serve immediately garnished with roasted peanuts.

⊥ Date Honey Banana Shake ⊥

This energy filled shake is a great way to start your day. If you are hungry and not in a mood to cook, you will get all the nutrients if you have one serving of this revitalizer.

Preparation time : 15 minutes.   Cooking time : 5 minutes.   Serves 1.

¼ cup deseeded dates (khajur)
1 tbsp honey
½ banana
1 cup milk
4 to 6 ice-cubes

1. Heat the milk and soak the dates in it for 10 to 15 minutes till they soften and the milk is cold.
2. Combine the soaked dates, milk, banana and honey with ice-cubes and blend in a liquidiser.
   Serve immediately.

⋏ Magaz ⋏

A mouthwatering delicacy that simply melts in your mouth. The combination of besan with sugar and ghee loads this dish with enough energy to satiate hunger pangs and help overcome fatigue. Have one piece and you will feel recharged.

Preparation time : 10 minutes. Cooking time : 15 minutes. Makes 10 pieces.

1 cup Bengal gram flour (besan)
½ cup powdered sugar
½ tsp cardamom (elaichi) powder
a pinch nutmeg (jaiphal) powder
1 tbsp slivered almonds (badam)
⅓ cup ghee

1. Heat the ghee in a non-stick pan and add the besan when the ghee melts.
2. Cook them together over a slow flame stirring continuously till the besan is golden brown.
3. Remove from the flame and transfer into a bowl. Allow it to cool completely.
4. Add the sugar, cardamom powder and nutmeg powder and mix well using your hands.

5. Divide the mixture into 10 equal portions and shape each portion into round balls.
6. Garnish with slivered almonds and store in an air-tight container.

11. FEVER

What is fever?

Fever is a rise in the body temperature above normal levels i.e. above 36.9°C or 98.4°F. It can present itself with various ailments like viral infections, allergy and other diseases like jaundice, chicken pox, malaria etc.

Remedies

The remedies mentioned below are ones that can be put to use only when fever is a result of a viral infection, exhaustion or because of some other ailments like chicken pox, malaria etc.

➤ **Tulsi (Indian basil):** A mixture made by grinding few tulsi leaves, ¼ tsp of sunflower seeds (surya mukhi ke beej) and 1 tsp of honey helps to overcome fever.

➤ **Mint (phudina) and ginger (adrak):** Any type of fever can be cured quickly by drinking the mint and ginger concoction. See recipe of *Fresh Herbal Cup, page 80*.

➤ **Turmeric powder (haldi):** Half a tsp of turmeric powder and a quarter tsp of black pepper powder mixed in a cup of hot milk has been proven to be excellent for fever. Drink this milk twice a day.

➤ **Sandalwood:** Applying sandalwood mixture on the forehead also helps to reduce the body temperature.

Foods to be Avoided
✧ Chilled beverages and ice-creams
✧ Deep fried foods
✧ Confectionery and mithai

Tips to Hasten Recovery from Fever
1. Consume plenty of green leafy vegetables (cabbage, spinach, broccoli), sprouts and red and yellow fruits and vegetables (oranges, tomatoes, carrots etc.) which abound in vitamins A, B complex, C, zinc and iron.
2. Drink of plenty of fluids (water, soups and juices) as this helps to replenish the fluids lost during infection. You can also try the *Spicy Masala Tea, page 81*, to make up for your body fluids and to chase away the cough and cold that usually accompanies the fever.

3. Eat freshly cooked meals instead of refrigerated foods.
4. Avoid foods that put a strain on your body's metabolism like oily foods.
5. Avoid smoking as it aggravates the throat and interferes with the infection-fighting activity of the cells.
6. Take plenty of rest as it gives your body a better chance to fight the virus.

⋏ Fresh Herbal Cup ⋏

This herb packed and honey combed hot drink is just perfect to perk up your spirits during fever.

Preparation time : 5 minutes.   Cooking time : 7 minutes.   Makes 2 cups.

¼ cup chopped mint (phudina)
25 mm. (1") piece ginger (adrak), chopped
¼ cup chopped tulsi leaves
1½ cups water
1 to 2 tbsp honey

1. Grind the mint, ginger and tulsi leaves in a blender.
2. Add water to it and boil it for 5 to 7 minutes.
3. Strain and drink while it is still warm.

⊥ **Spicy Masala Tea** ⊥

All of us enjoy having tea. There can be nothing more pleasing during a cold than a hot cup of masala tea.

Preparation time : 10 minutes.   Cooking time : 20 minutes.   Serves 2.

2 to 3 stalks lemon grass (hare chai ki patti)
4 to 6 mint (phudina) leaves
½ tsp chai ka masala (recipe overleaf)
1 tsp grated ginger
2 tbsp sugar
1 cup milk

1. Combine the lemon grass, mint leaves and sugar with 2 cups of water and bring to a boil.
2. Simmer for 5 to 10 minutes till the aroma is released and the water is reduced to half.
3. Add the tea masala and bring it to a boil.
4. Add the milk and simmer for 4 to 5 minutes. Strain and serve hot.

⊼ Chai ka Masala ⊼

This chai ka masala added either to milk or tea is great to chase fever and cure sore throat.

Preparation time : 10 minutes   Cooking time : 10 minutes   Makes 1 cup.

¼ cup cinnamon (dalchini), cut into small pieces
⅛ cup cloves (laung)
¼ cup black peppercorns
¼ cup cardamom (elaichi)
6 black cardamom (moti elaichi)
¼ cup mace (javantri), broken into pieces
½ nutmeg (jaiphal), grated
¼ cup ginger powder (soonth)

1. Dry roast the cinnamon, cloves, black pepper, cardamom and black cardamom for 7 to 8 minutes. Cool completely.
2. Add the mace, nutmeg and ginger powder and grind to make a fine powder.
3. Cool completely and store in an air-tight container.
   Use as required.

12. HEADACHE

Headache occurs to each individual at some time or the other.

What causes Headaches ?
It has many causes which are physiological or psychological, some of which are listed below.

✧ Hypoglycemia i.e. low blood sugar levels due to non-consumption of food
✧ Stress
✧ Allergies
✧ Excessive strain on eyes
✧ Lack of vitamins and minerals in the body leading to physical weakness that manifests itself in the form of a headache
✧ Other illness like sinusitis

Remedies

➢ **Lemon:** An equal proportion of lemon and ginger juice when consumed brings instant relief from headache. Try the recipe of *Ginger and Lemon Cup, page 86*, to overcome headache.

- **Turmeric milk:** One tsp of turmeric powder mixed in a glass of milk and boiled for 5 to 10 minutes is an effective remedy against headache.

- **Tulsi (Indian basil):** Tulsi in combination with lemon is an age-old remedy for headache.

- **Cinnamon (dalchini):** A paste made with cinnamon and water should be applied on the forehead 2 to 3 times every day.

- **Ginger (adrak):** One tbsp of ginger juice combined with ½ tbsp of Tulsi juice should be used as nose drops to relieve headache.

- **Cloves (laung):** A fine mixture of cloves and salt with water or milk is a common cure for headache. Apply the mixture on the forehead twice or thrice daily.

Foods to be Avoided
- Tea and coffee
- Fermented foods like dhokla, idli, dosa, cheese etc.
- Chilled beverages and ice-creams
- Pickles and preserved foods
- Chocolates

A Few Ways to Chase a Headache Away

The best therapy for a headache is one that suits the malady that it comes with. Here are a few ways that work well for most headaches.

1. Try and restrict the consumption of sugar. Though sugar in small quantities actually helps to cure headaches, excess sugar may trigger a headache or sometimes worsen an already existing one.
2. Consume plenty of fresh fruits and vegetables as they abound in vitamins A, C, E and B complex, zinc and iron all of which strengthen the immune system. Sources of these vitamins include green leafy vegetables (cabbage, spinach, broccoli), sprouts and red and yellow fruits and vegetables (tomato, orange, sweet lime, carrot etc.).
3. Avoid smoking as it can aggravate the headache.
4. Indulge in any activity you enjoy. Listen to music, go for a walk or cook as it keeps our mind and body fresh and alert.
5. A stress related headache will vanish with a warm oil head massage accompanied with a glass of warm *Kashmiri Kahwa, page 87.*

⁂ Ginger and Lemon Cup ⁂

This drink can never fail to overcome headache.
I have added glucose powder to this drink as it provides the much needed
excess calories for anorexics.
To extract ginger juice, grate ginger and squeeze out the juice from the pulp.

Preparation time : 5 minutes.   No cooking.   Makes 1 cup.

2 tsp lemon juice
2 tsp ginger (adrak) juice
1 tbsp glucose powder
1 cup water
a pinch black salt (sanchal)

Mix all the ingredients and serve immediately.

⅄ Kashmiri Kahwa ⅄

Cloves, cinnamon and ginger — the 3 ingredients used is this recipe mixed with Kashmiri green tea and flavoured with cardamom is what helps you relieve headache and maintain fluid levels too.
Kashmiri green tea is available at most food stores and selected provision stores.

Preparation time : A few minutes.   Boiling time : 10 minutes.   Serves 4.

4 tsp Kashmiri green tea
1 stick cinnamon (dalchini)
2 cardamoms (elaichi), slightly crushed
2 cloves (laung)
2 tbsp sugar
4 pinches saffron
8 almonds (badam), blanched and chopped

1. Boil 3 cups of water along with cinnamon, cardamom, cloves and sugar and pour over the tea. Leave to infuse over a very low flame for 2 to 3 minutes.
2. Meanwhile, dissolve saffron in a little water by rubbing it gently.
3. Strain the tea and add the saffron liquid together with almonds. Serve hot.

13. HIGH BLOOD CHOLESTEROL LEVELS / HEART DISEASE

What is Cholesterol?

Cholesterol is a yellowish fatty substance in our blood that is essential in small quantities. Excessive cholesterol can however block the arteries leading to reduced blood supply which causes slow damage to the heart causing various types of heart diseases.

Causes of High Blood Cholesterol

✧ Heredity
✧ Excessive consumption of sugar and fat
✧ Lack of exercise
✧ Smoking
✧ Other illness like diabetes, high blood pressure etc.

Remedies

➤ **Fibre rich fruits and vegetables:** Fruits and vegetables like orange, guava, cluster beans (gavarfali), green peas, unpeeled carrot etc. help to keep the blood cholesterol levels at bay due to their high fibre content. So, have plenty of raw fruits and vegetables in your daily diet. Try the recipe of *Muesli, page 92*, made with a combination of fruits and high fibre cereals like corn flakes and oats.

➤ **Garlic (lehsun):** 1 to 2 cloves of garlic has been proven to reduce the cholesterol levels in the blood thereby preventing the hardening of arteries. Though the earlier damage may not be repaired, the chances of a new heart attack do decrease. Try the recipe of *Carrot Garlic Chutney, page 94*, for a flavourful way to add raw garlic to your diet daily.

➤ **Onion (pyaz):** Raw onions contain certain beneficials that are helpful in reducing bad cholestrol levels. One should try and have at least one raw onion everyday in salads along with meals for optimum benefits.

➤ **Amla (Indian gooseberry):** Dried amla powder strengthens the organs of our body including the heart. Dry the amlas and grind into a fine powder. One tsp of this powder with a glass of warm water helps to strengthen the heart.

➤ **Arjuna (kahu):** The preparation made from the bark of arjuna is known to have a stimulating effect on the heart and is used as a tonic for the heart. A decoction made with the thick portion of the bark boiled in hot water should be taken on an empty stomach every morning. The bark of arjuna looks like cinnamon (dalchini) but is larger and thicker and can be reused at least for 3 to 4 times. Alternatively, 1 gram of powder of this bark can also be consumed with a cup of warm milk. It is easily available at ayurvedic stores.

Foods to be Avoided
✧ Full fat dairy products
✧ Sweeteners like sugar, jaggery and honey
✧ Deep fried foods
✧ Confectionery and mithai
✧ Pickles, canned and preserved foods
✧ Refined foods like maida, sugar, pasta and polished rice
✧ Fast foods like pizzas, burgers etc.
✧ Creamy salad dressings
✧ Aerated drinks

Ways to Maintain Blood Cholesterol Levels
1. Choose oil instead of ghee in your daily cooking, as the latter is one of the major causes of high blood cholesterol. Restrict your consumption of fat to 3 tsp per day.
2. Have plenty of onions and garlic as a part of your two major meals lunch and dinner, to control your blood cholesterol levels.

3. Choose whole grains like whole wheat flour, oats, bajra, jowar etc. over refined cereals like maida, semolina etc. as the former abounds in fibre which helps to decrease blood cholesterol levels. Try the *Stuffed Bajre ki Roti, page 95,* as it's an interesting way of adding fibre to your meals.
4. Replace full fat dairy products with their low fat counterparts.
5. Indulge in an exercise programme regularly. It helps improve blood circulation and also destroys the excess bad cholesterol.

⋏ Muesli ⋏

This fruit and oat porridge with low fat milk makes a hearty and high fibre breakfast that helps to keep a close check on blood cholesterol levels. Have this daily and make a great beginning everyday.

Preparation time : 5 minutes.   Cooking time : 10 minutes.   Makes 3½ cups.

2 cups cornflakes
1 cup quick cooking rolled oats
4 tbsp wheat bran
¼ tsp vanilla essence
3 tbsp raisins (kismish)

For serving
low fat milk
few pieces of chopped apples

1. Combine the oats and wheat bran and lightly toast them in a non-stick pan over a slow flame for 5 to 7 minutes.

2. Cool completely, add the cornflakes, vanilla essence and sultanas. Mix well. Store in an air-tight container.
3. For serving, place ¼ of the muesli into a individual bowl with the apples and pour the milk on top.
   Serve immediately.

⋏ Carrot Garlic Chutney ⋏

This chutney is a great way of including fibre rich carrot and cholesterol lowering garlic to your meals. However, it is wise to avoid this chutney if a heart patient is hypertensive too.

Preparation time: 30 minutes.   No cooking.   Makes ½ cup.

1 cup thickly grated carrot
2 tbsp chopped garlic (lehsun)
2 tsp chilli powder
¼ tsp lemon juice
1 tsp oil
1 tsp salt

1. Grind the garlic, chilli powder, lemon juice and salt to a fine paste in a blender.
2. Combine the carrots, garlic paste and oil in a bowl and mix well.
    Serve immediately.

Handy tip : The chutney will stay well, if refrigerated, for upto 4 days.

⋏ Stuffed Bajre ki Roti ⋏

High fibre bajra rotis stuffed with chawli (long beans) that are flavoured with garlic make a meal in itself. Whole wheat flour is added to the bajra flour to make it easier to roll out the rotis. Enjoy these stuffed rotis for breakfast, lunch or dinner, served with low fat curds or Carrot Garlic Chutney, page 94.

Preparation time: 15 minutes.   Cooking time: 10 minutes.   Makes 2 rotis.

For the bajra rotis
½ cup bajra flour (black millet flour)
2 tbsp whole wheat flour (gehun ka atta)
salt to taste

For the stuffing
1 cup chopped chawli (long beans)
3 to 4 green chillies, chopped
1 tbsp chopped garlic (lehsun)
2 tbsp chopped coriander
a pinch asafoetida (hing)
1 tsp oil

salt to taste

For the bajra rotis
1. Mix the bajra flour, wheat flour and salt and enough hot water to make a soft dough.
2. Knead well. Divide the dough into 4 equal portions.
3. Roll out each portion of the dough thinly into circles of 200 mm. (8") diameter.
4. Lightly cook the bajra rotis on a non-stick pan on both sides.

For the stuffing
1. Combine the chawli, green chillies, garlic and coriander in a blender or food processor without using any water to make a coarse paste.
2. Heat the oil in a non-stick pan, add the asafoetida, salt and the ground chawli mixture and sauté for 3 to 4 minutes till the chawli is tender.
3. Cool and divide the mixture into 2 portions.

How to proceed
1. Spread one portion of the filling on one cooked bajra roti. Then place another bajra roti on top and press the sides so that the filling is sealed between the two rotis.
2. Cook the stuffed roti on a non-stick pan over a slow flame, till both sides are golden brown.
3. Repeat for the remaining ingredients to make 1 more roti.
   Serve hot with Carrot Garlic Chutney and low fat curds.

14. HIGH BLOOD PRESSURE (HYPERTENSION)

What is High Blood Pressure?

High blood pressure or hypertension is a condition in which the blood pressure goes above the normal level of 120/80.

The main causes of High Blood Pressure are

- ✧ Obesity
- ✧ Smoking
- ✧ Excessive intake of salt
- ✧ Stress
- ✧ Narrowing of arteries due to high cholesterol

Symptoms of High Blood Pressure

- ✧ Headache and / or dizziness
- ✧ Impaired vision
- ✧ Unexplained tiredness
- ✧ Pain in the chest

Remedies

- **Garlic (lehsun):** One to two cloves of garlic taken on an empty stomach in the morning daily is the best remedy to control high blood pressure.

- **Amla (Indian gooseberry):** An effective treatment for high blood pressure is a mixture made with equal amounts of amla juice and honey. Have a tbsp of this mixture early in the morning every day.

- **Low sodium fruits and vegetables:** Fruits and vegetables like orange, guava, sweet lime, plums, cucumber, green peas, french beans, ladies finger, brinjal, bitter gourd etc. help to keep high blood pressure at bay. If you are not very fond of these raw fruits and vegetables, try their juices and soups instead. See the recipe of *Garlic Vegetable Soup, page 101*.

- **Fluids:** Drink plenty of fluids to maintain the fluid and electrolyte (sodium and potassium) balance in the blood.

- **Salt substitutes:** Restrict the consumption of salt to keep a check on your blood pressure. Instead, try natural salt substitutes like black salt or use herbs and spices like chilli, pepper or home made *Sesame Herb Blend, page 103*, to minimize the daily intake of salt and add more flavours to your meals.

Foods to be Avoided

- ✧ Full fat dairy products
- ✧ Dried fruits and nuts especially salted
- ✧ Sweeteners like sugar, jaggery and honey
- ✧ Deep fried foods
- ✧ Confectionery and mithai
- ✧ Pickles, papads, canned and preserved foods
- ✧ Refined foods like maida, sugar, pasta and polished rice
- ✧ Fast foods like pizzas, burgers etc.
- ✧ Creamy salad dressings
- ✧ Aerated drinks
- ✧ Ready-to-eat snacks like wafers, popcorn etc.
- ✧ Ajinomoto (monosodium glutamate)

Pointers for Keeping High Blood Pressure in Check

- ✧ Restrict the consumption of green leafy vegetables to minimum, as these are rich in sodium.
- ✧ Have plenty of whole grains and pulses in your meals as these are low in sodium.
- ✧ Salt has a tendency to increase the blood pressure instantaneously. So, it's important to curtail the intake of salt as per your doctor's advise. It is advisable to avoid foods like papads, pickles, canned foods etc. due to their high sodium content.

- ✧ Use oil instead of ghee in your daily cooking, as the latter is one of the major causes of high blood cholesterol. Restrict the consumption of fat to 3 tsp per day.
- ✧ Replace full fat dairy products with their low fat counterparts.

⌃ Garlic Vegetable Soup ⌃

*A garlic flavoured vegetable soup thickened with oats. Both vegetables
and oats are high in fibre.*

Preparation time : 10 minutes.   Cooking time : 15 minutes.   Serves 2.

1 cup finely chopped mixed vegetables (carrots, French beans, cauliflower, peas, baby corn)
2 tsp finely chopped garlic
¼ cup finely chopped onions
2 tbsp quick cooking rolled oats
1 tsp oil
salt and pepper to taste

For the garnish
2 tbsp chopped coriander

1. Heat the oil in a pan, add the onions and garlic and sauté till the onions are translucent.
2. Add the vegetables and sauté for a few minutes.

101

3. Add 2 cups of water, salt and pepper. Allow it to come to a boil and simmer till the vegetables are tender.
4. Add the oats and simmer for another 5 minutes.
   Serve hot garnished with chopped coriander.

⅄ Sesame Herb Blend ⅄

Kiss your salt cellars goodbye. This natural herb and spice blend is all set to win your heart over.

Preparation time: A few minutes.   No cooking. Makes ½ cup (approx.).

5 tsp dehydrated onion flakes, lightly toasted
1½ tsp garlic (lehsun) powder
6 tsp sesame seeds (til), lightly roasted
2 Kashmiri chillies, lightly roasted
2 tsp oregano
2 pinches citric acid crystals
½ tsp salt (optional)

Mix all the ingredients and blend in a blender to get a fine powder. Store in an air-tight container. Use as required.

15. INSOMNIA

What is Insomnia?

In simple terms, insomnia is lack of sleep. Insomnia deprives a person of mental rest and thereby interferes with one's day-to-day activities. It is most commonly experienced in old age.

What are the Reasons for Insomnia?

✧ Insomnia attacks those who are extremely hyper or are stressed and over exerted. On the other extreme, even those who do not have a very active lifestyle can be insomniacs.

✧ Lack of physical activity.

✧ Lack of nutrients due to an unbalanced diet.

✧ Constipation, overeating, anger and mental tension are some other causes of sleepless nights.

Remedies

Try one of the following remedies before going to bed to enjoy a peaceful night of restful sleep.

➤ **Milk:** A glass of milk with or without honey mixed with turmeric powder taken just before going to bed daily is the best remedy for insomnia. Try *Soothing Sleep Inducer, page 107,* for all-in-one remedy to insomnia.

➢ **Curds (dahi):** Consume plenty of curds throughout the day. This helps in inducing sleep.

➢ **Onion (pyaz):** Consumption of raw onion at dinner time helps to overcome restless nights.

➢ **Nutmeg (jaiphal):** Nutmeg powder mixed with water is an effective remedy for insomnia.

➢ **Khus-khus (poppy seeds):** A paste made with 2 grams of khus-khus, ½ tsp of sugar and ½ tsp of honey should be taken at night for curing insomnia.

Foods to be Avoided
✧ Tea and coffee
✧ Aerated drinks
✧ Canned and preserved foods
✧ Deep fried foods
✧ Confectionery and mithai
✧ Spicy and strong flavoured foods especially before going to bed

7 Sleep Inducers

1. Adhere to a regular sleeping schedule, going to bed at a fixed time each night and getting up at a fixed time every morning. Early to bed and early to rise is a good rule.
2. Take a warm bath just before going to bed. Wear loose clothing and curl up with a relaxing book to unwind and induce restful sleep.
3. Try and avoid smoking and caffeinated beverages as they can make you more hyper and retard relaxation.
4. Consume plenty of fruits and vegetables in any form as deficiencies of nutrients often lead to lack of sleep. An easy way to meet your nutrient requirement is to make salads a part of both your major meals — lunch and dinner.
5. Limit liquids of any kind for at least 1½ hours before bedtime as the need to urinate may wake you up in the middle of the night and break your restful sleep. It takes about 90 minutes for the body to process liquids. This problem is faced especially in older people.
6. Controlled breathing is also a great help in inducing sleep. The method is to lie on your side in bed and then take three deep breaths expanding the abdomen completely. Then hold your breath as long as you can. Holding the breath leads to accumulation of carbon dioxide which induces sleep.
7. Regular, active exercising during the day and mild exercise at bedtime enhances the duration and the quality of sleep.

⚔ Soothing Sleep Inducer ⚔

This milk flavoured with powdered herbs and spices from different parts of India is sure to help overcome insomnia especially after a warm bath.

Preparation time : 10 minutes.   Cooking time : 10 minutes.   Makes 1 cup.

For the masala powder
¼ cup khus-khus (poppy seeds) toasted
¼ cup almonds (badam), toasted
½ nutmeg (jaiphal), chopped
½ tsp turmeric powder (haldi)

For the milk
1 tbsp masala powder, recipe above
1 tbsp honey or jaggery (gur)
1 cup milk

For the masala powder
1. Combine the khus-khus, almonds and nutmeg and grind it to obtain a fine powder.
2. Add the turmeric powder and mix well. Store in an air-tight container.

Use as required.

How to proceed
Bring the milk to a boil and add the masala powder and the honey. Mix well.
Serve hot.

Handy tip: The masala mixture can be stored refrigerated in an air-tight container for upto a month.

16. PIMPLE / ACNE

What is a Pimple / Acne?

A pimple or acne is a small swelling on the skin containing pus, usually on the face and neck. It usually occurs around puberty.

Causes for the Formation of Pimple / Acne

- ✧ Acne can be a result of hormonal changes during adolescence, skin allergies or even constipation.
- ✧ Faulty selection of foods like excessive consumption of starch, sugar or fat in the diet, irregular eating habits.
- ✧ Deficiency of vitamin A and zinc are also one of the most prevalent causes of acne/pimples.
- ✧ An oily complexion and pollution can worsen the problem.

Remedies

➤ **Black raisins:** A sherbet made with black raisins, sugar and fennel seeds (saunf) helps to bring quick results as it cleans the digestive tract and chases body heat away. See the recipe of *Fruitful Healer, page 112.*

➤ **Fruits and vegetables:** Fruits and vegetables like cucumber, oranges, watermelon, papaya, chickoo, mint, spinach etc. are rich in fibre and nutrients like vitamin A, vitamin C and vitamin E which help to have a glowing skin. Include the *Cooling Cucumber Raita, page 113,* in your meals every day and you will see the results yourselves.

➤ **Multani mitti (Fuller's Earth), rose water and sandalwood paste:** A paste made with equal proportions of these three ingredients when applied on the face for 15 to 20 minutes will rejuvenate acne prone oily skin.

➤ **Tomato:** Rub a slice of a ripe tomato over the skin. Dry it for ½ hour and wash off with lukewarm water.

➤ **Tulsi (Indian basil):** Applying a mixture of juice of tulsi with lemon or ginger (adrak) will also help to cure pimples with its scars.

Foods to be Avoided

✧ Tea and coffee

- ✧ Spicy and oily foods
- ✧ Confectionery and mithai
- ✧ Full fat dairy products
- ✧ Pickles, canned and preserved foods
- ✧ Refined foods like maida, sugar, pasta and polished rice
- ✧ Creamy salad dressings

Suggestions for a Glowing Complexion

1. Wash your skin gently twice daily with an antibacterial soap (not regular soap) as it is alkaline and will retard bacterial growth. Washing will keep the pores open and your skin free of bacteria. However, don't scrub too hard, as this will irritate your skin further.
2. Keep your hands away from your face or other affected areas. They may contain oils and bacteria that could promote acne. Wash your hands frequently.
3. Avoid greasy creams and cosmetics, especially ones that contain oils and dyes.
4. Include sprouts and fruits as a part of your daily diet.
5. Reduce the consumption of junk foods, sugar and limit your total fat intake to no more than 4 tsp per day.
6. Drink plenty of water and have a regular regime for exercise as this helps to flush the system.

⋏ Fruitful Healer ⋏

This sweet preparation is sure to tantalize your taste buds and give you a pimple free smooth skin too. Consuming this drink regularly even after the pimples disappear, will help you to gain a glowing complexion.

Preparation time : 10 minutes.   No cooking.   Makes 1 cup.

1 tbsp black raisins (kismis)
1 tbsp fennel seeds (saunf)
1 tbsp sugar
1 cup water

1. Combine all the ingredients and soak for at least 4 to 6 hours.
2. Liquidise in a blender and drink immediately.

⅄ Cooling Cucumber Raita ⅄

Like most fresh uncooked food, this mint flavoured cucumber raita packs in a loads of nutrients and hence good for your skin. You can even blend this in a liquidiser to make an innovative chaas.

Preparation time: 10 minutes.   No cooking.   Serves 4.

2 small cucumbers, chopped
3 to 4 tbsp chopped mint (phudina) leaves
2 cups curds
½ tsp roasted cumin seed (jeera) powder
salt to taste

1. Whisk the curds until smooth.
2. Add the cucumber, mint leaves, cumin seed powder and salt and mix well.
3. Refrigerate till chilled.
   Serve with rice or parathas.

▲ Orange Revitalizer ▲

Tropical fruit juice laced with coconut milk. The high vitamin C content of this refreshing drink fights against acne and keeps your skin looking great.

Preparation time : A few minutes.   No cooking.   Serves 2.

4 to 5 tbsp grated coconut
1½ cups papaya pieces
¾ cup fresh orange juice
2 tsp sugar
8 ice-cubes

1. Mix the coconut with 1 tbsp of water in a blender.
2. Place over a piece of fine cloth and squeeze out thick coconut milk.
3. Blend the papaya pieces, orange juice, sugar, coconut milk and ice-cubes in a blender till smooth.
4. Pour into individual glasses. Serve immediately with crushed ice.

17. PROTEIN DEFICIENCY

Protein is essential in our diet as it carries out an important function of repair and maintenance of body cells and tissues. A deficiency of protein can lead to impaired growth in children and general deterioration in adults. A balanced diet should provide 15 to 20% of our daily calories from protein.

Ways to Detect Protein Deficiency

❖ Weight loss
❖ Anaemia (Iron deficiency)
❖ Swollen abdomen
❖ Greying of hair
❖ Slow healing of wounds
❖ Decreased resistance to diseases
❖ Muscular pain
❖ Overall retarded growth

Remedies

Here are some protein packed ingredients which are sure to help you raise your protein levels.

> **Dairy products:** Dairy products like milk, curds, paneer and buttermilk are the richest sources of protein.

> **Dals and pulses:** Dals and pulses like moong dal, rajma, soyabean, toovar dal etc. are extremely good sources of protein. Consume at least 2 cups of any of the cooked dals or pulses to cure protein deficiency quickly. These dals and pulses if consumed in combination with cereals like wheat, bajra, jowar, ragi etc. make a complete protein in itself. Idli and khichdi are the most common dishes made with a combination of rice (a cereal) and dal (a pulse). See the healthy version of *Nutritious Idlis, page 118.*

> **Sprouts:** Sprouts are extremely good sources of protein. Sprouting not only makes the digestion easy but also increases the nutrient content. If you are not very fond of sprouts, try the mouth-watering recipe of *Usli, page 119.*

> **Nuts and oilseeds:** Nuts and oilseeds like cashewnuts (kaju), almonds (badam), sesame seeds (til), groundnuts etc. are also good sources of protein. However, keep in mind that nuts and oilseeds in excess amounts are not healthy due to their high saturated fatty acids. So we must indulge in them sensibly.

Foods to be Avoided

◇ Tea and coffee
◇ Refined foods like maida, sugar, pasta and polished rice
◇ Aerated drinks

Enhance the Intake of Protein in the Following Ways

1. Have small and frequent meals equally distributed throughout the day as protein deficient individuals are often seen to have lower appetite.
2. Have dals and pulses for both the major meals of the day.
3. Consume 2 to 3 glasses of milk in any form to overcome protein deficiency.
4. Include plenty of fruits and vegetables in your daily diet as protein deficiency is usually accompanied by other nutrient deficiencies too.

⋏ Nutritious Idlis ⋏

An extremely popular South Indian dish that is a perfect example of a complete protein combination which combines a cereal (rice) and a pulse (moong dal).

Preparation time : 10 minutes.   Cooking time : 15 minutes.   Makes 8 idlis.

½ cup rice
½ cup green moong dal (split green gram)
½ tsp fenugreek (methi) seeds (optional)
salt to taste

1. Soak the rice, dal and fenugreek seeds in water for 5 to 6 hours.
2. Grind the soaked ingredients in a mixer and leave the batter aside for at least 8 hours or preferably overnight.
3. Thereafter, add the salt and pour a little mixture into the cavities of a small idli maker.
4. Steam in a cooker for a few minutes. Repeat for the remaining mixture.
   Serve hot with chutney and sambhar.

⊥ Usli ⊥

Usli is a mixture of healthy stir-fried sprouts. Sprouting not only kills the anti-nutritional factors in the pulses but also enhances their nutrient content and makes them more digestible.

Preparation time : 10 minutes.   Cooking time : 10 minutes.   Serves 4.

¾ cup sprouted moong (whole green gram)
⅓ cup sprouted red chana
⅓ cup sprouted chick peas (kabuli chana)
⅓ cup sprouted peanuts
1 tsp cumin seeds (jeera)
½ cup chopped onions
½ tsp chopped ginger (adrak)
4 cloves garlic, chopped
2 green chillies, chopped
½ cup chopped tomatoes
¼ tsp turmeric powder (haldi)
1 tbsp chopped coriander
½ tsp chilli powder

1 cup boiled and chopped potatoes
1 tsp lemon juice
2 tsp oil
salt to taste

1. Boil the moong sprouts, red chana sprouts, chick pea sprouts and sprouted peanuts till they are tender. Do not cook in a pressure cooker. Drain and keep aside.
2. Heat the oil in a tava (griddle) and add the cumin seeds.
3. When they crackle, add the onions and sauté for a few seconds.
4. Add the ginger, garlic and green chillies and fry again for a few seconds.
5. Add the tomatoes, turmeric powder, coriander and chilli powder and fry again for a while.
6. Add the potatoes, drained sprouts, lemon juice and salt. Mix well.
   Serve hot.

18. SORE THROAT / THROAT PAIN

What is Sore Throat?

Sore throat is inflammation (infection) of the throat.

Causes of Sore Throat

- ◇ Infection like a cold and cough
- ◇ Pollution
- ◇ Change of weather

Remedies

Though there is not much one can do to make it disappear at will, these remedies are sure to make your throat feel a lot better.

➤ **Salt water gargle:** Gargling with warm water made by dissolving two to three pinches of salt is a tried and tested remedy. Repeat this as often as possible for a speedy recovery.

➤ **Clove (laung):** Two to three lightly roasted cloves should be kept in the mouth. The oils released from the cloves help to soothe the throat and also keeps your breath fresh.

➤ **Cinnamon (dalchini):** Add a tsp of cinnamon powder and a tsp of honey to a cup of warm water and sip on it.

➤ **Lemon:** Combine the juice of ½ lemon with 1 tsp of honey in a cup of hot water and sip it while it is still warm. Repeat this at least two or three times a day.

➤ **Ajwain (carom seeds):** A quarter to half tsp of ajwain mixed in warm milk helps to ease the sore throat. Check out the recipe of *Ajwain and Turmeric Milk, page124*.

➤ **Tulsi (Indian basil):** A concoction made by boiling basil leaves in water is a very well known remedy for sore throat. See the recipe of *Tulsi Tea, page 125*.

Foods to be Avoided
✧ Spicy, oily and salty foods
✧ Aerated drinks
✧ Deep fried foods
✧ Ice-creams

◇ Confectionery and mithai
◇ Canned and preserved foods

Easy Tips for Soothing a Sore Throat

1. Try to serve foods at room temperature or lukewarm as hot food may cause throat irritation.
2. Have semi-liquid and soft foods which do not require much chewing. However eat enough to meet up your daily nutrient requirement. For example, a bland khichdi, a milk shake, roti dipped in dal are all good choices to ease a sore throat.
3. Do not eat meals in a hurry as this may be irritating for the throat. Sit down in one place and eat in a calm and relaxed atmosphere.
4. Avoid smoking as it aggravates the throat and interferes with the infection-fighting activity of the cells.
5. REST a lot as it gives your body a better chance to fight off the virus.

⊿ Ajwain and Turmeric Milk ⊿

An age-old remedy for cough. Two glasses of this milk a day taken for 2 to 3 days is sure to chase away cough and ease a sore throat.

Preparation time : 5 minutes.   Cooking time : 5 minutes.   Serves 1.

¼ tsp ajwain (carom seeds)
a large pinch turmeric powder (haldi)
1 cup milk
2 tsp sugar (optional)

1. Heat the milk with the sugar in a pan and keep aside.
2. In a non-stick pan, heat the ajwain and stir it continuously till it is almost browned.
3. Add the turmeric powder and stir it for another second or so.
4. Add the warm milk to the ajwain and turmeric powder and mix well.
5. Pour into a glass and serve immediately.

⏶ Tulsi Tea ⏶

Hot tea made with natural ingredients like tulsi and lemon is extremely soothing for the throat as the leaves of tulsi help to fight off the germs.

Preparation time : 3 minutes.   Cooking time : 10 minutes.   Makes 1 cup.

10 to 15 tulsi (basil) leaves
juice of 1 lemon

1. Add the basil leaves in 1½ cups of water.
2. Boil for 10 minutes.
3. Strain and add the lemon juice.
   Serve warm.

19. STOMACHACHE / INDIGESTION

What is a Stomachache?

Stomachache is the abdominal discomfort caused due to pain in the stomach or abdomen.

Reasons for Stomachache

Stomachache can occur for a number of reasons. A few of the most common causes are :

✧ Overeating and indigestion
✧ Stomach infection (caused due to bacteria / amoeba etc.)
✧ Acidity
✧ Flatulence (gas)
✧ Constipation

Remedies

The number of remedies for this ailment are as many as the number of reasons that can lead to stomachache. Here are some remedies that are tried and tested over generations. Select one that is appropriate for you.

> **Ginger (adrak):** Mix 2 tsp of ginger juice with 1 tsp of lemon juice and a pinch of salt and black pepper and drink it with or without water.

> **Ajwain (carom seeds):** One tsp of ajwain combined with 2 pinches of salt should be chewed and swallowed for relief from flatulence.

> **Mint (phudina):** The juice of mint combined with honey is one of the age-old remedies for stomachache. Refer to the recipe of *Lemon Phudina Pani, page 67,* for instant relief.

> **Ginger powder (soonth) and jaggery (gur):** The *Tummy Reliever, page 131,* is soothing for your stomach and also helps to keep your spirits warm in cold weather. Mountaineers carry this magic portion to keep their strength up in the harsh mountain terrain.

Foods to be Avoided

- ✧ Spicy and oily foods
- ✧ Deep fried foods
- ✧ Aerated drinks
- ✧ Fast foods like pizza, burger etc.
- ✧ Refined foods like maida, sugar, pasta and polished rice
- ✧ Canned and preserved foods

Handy Hints to Cure Stomachache

1. Have plenty of fluids. *Digestive Soda, page 132* and *Lemon and Coriander Soup, page 129,* are flavourful variations to help relieve stomachache.
2. Have small and frequent freshly cooked meals throughout the day as it aids in digestion.
3. Eat easily digestible foods. Consume foods that are liquid or semi-liquid in consistency.
4. Have plenty of fibre as it initiates regular bowel movements. Fibre rich foods include fruits, vegetables and whole grains like whole wheat, wheat bran, oats, buckwheat etc.
5. Restrict the consumption of fat to a minimum as fat takes a long time to digest.
6. Chew the food slowly and eat in a relaxed environment as sometimes tensions and stress tend to upset the tummy.
7. Avoid eating in an unhygienic environment.

Lemon and Coriander Soup

An aromatic and healthy soup. This is an interesting deviation from the regular clear vegetable soup. Fragrant lemon grass makes this clear soup very appetizing and the coriander lends its own distinct flavour and colour.

Preparation time : 10 minutes. Cooking time : 15 minutes. Serves 4.

For the stock
2 to 3 pieces lemon grass, washed
1 to 2 green chillies, slit

Other ingredients
¼ cup sliced carrots
¼ cup sliced mushrooms
¼ cup finely chopped cabbage
2 spring onions, sliced
1 tsp oil
salt and pepper to taste

For the garnish
1 tbsp chopped coriander
1 tsp lemon juice

For the stock
1. Combine the lemon grass and green chillies in a pan with 6 cups of water and bring to a boil.
2. Simmer till it reduces to approx. 4 cups. Strain and keep the stock aside discarding the lemon grass and chillies.

How to proceed
1. Heat the oil in a pan, add the carrots, mushrooms, cabbage and spring onions and sauté for 1 to 2 minutes.
2. Add the stock, salt and pepper and bring to a boil.
3. Simmer till the vegetables are crunchy.
   Serve hot garnished with chopped coriander and lemon juice.

⋏ Tummy Reliever ⋏

An easy and effective remedy for stomachache due to indigestion or constipation.

Preparation time : 5 minutes.   No cooking.   Makes 12 portions.

2 tbsp ginger powder (soonth)
6 tbsp grated jaggery (gur)

1. Combine both the ingredients and mix well.
2. Divide into 12 equal portions and shape each portion into round balls.
3. Have 2 portions daily before going to bed.

⋏ Digestive Soda ⋏

Whip up this soda, drink it immediately and chase away the stomachache in minutes.

Preparation time : 5 minutes.   No cooking.   Makes 1 glass.

juice of 1 lemon
½ tsp freshly crushed pepper
½ tsp roasted cumin (jeera) powder
1 bottle (200 ml) soda water
salt to taste

1. Combine all the ingredients except the soda water in a tall glass.
2. Just before serving, add the soda water and drink it immediately before the fizz settles down.

20. SUNSTROKE

What is a Sunstroke?

It's a serious condition caused by excessive exposure to the hot sun which is characterized by dizziness, dehydration and a high body temperature but without prespiring. Constant exposure to excessive heat may also burn the topmost layer of skin which will eventually peel off.

Remedies

Try the following remedies if you ever experience sunstroke.

➤ **Raw Mango:** Raw mango is considered to be one of the most common cooling foods for sunstroke. *Panha, page 135,* a drink made with raw mango is most refreshing on a sunny afternoon.

➤ **Water rich fruits:** Consume plenty of water rich fruits like watermelon, pineapple, orange etc. These help to relieve excessive thirst and remove summer heat.

➤ **Fluids:** Drink plenty of fluids (water and fruit juices) to maintain your fluid and salt balance. Buttermilk made with fresh curds is considered to be one of the best fluids as it helps cool your system and relieves the heat from your body.

➤ **Onion:** Onions provide a cooling effect and it's good to have them raw in the form of salads or chutney for lunch everyday. You can also try the recipe of *Raw Mango and Onion Chutney, page 136.*

Foods to be Avoided
✧ Tea and coffee
✧ Nuts

Easy Ways to Relieve Sunstroke
1. If you happen to go out during sunny afternoons, use sunscreens and wear a hat. Also wear light weight natural fabrics to stay cool and protect your skin.
2. Apply a cool wash cloth to the upper spine and back to decrease body temperature.
3. Have plenty of fluids in the form of natural juices and avoid alcoholic, carbonated and caffienated drinks.
4. Take cool baths or showers at least 2 to 3 times a day.
5. Moisturize the skin to decrease body heat and also to ease sun-burnt skin.

⋏ Panha ⋏

A traditional summer drink that is very effective in fighting sun strokes.

Preparation time : 5 minutes.   Cooking time : 15 to 20 minutes.   Makes 4 to 6 glasses.

2 raw mangoes
¾ cup sugar
½ tsp cardamom (elaichi) powder
a few strands of saffron

1. Boil the raw mangoes in water till they are very soft.
2. Drain all the water and remove the skin from the mangoes.
3. Strain the mango pulp.
4. Add the sugar, cardamom powder and saffron and mix well.
5. Store in a bottle and refrigerate.
6. When you wish to serve, pour 2 tbsp of the mixture into a glass and top up with chilled water.

Handy tip : Instead of the cardamom and saffron, you can add cumin powder (jeera) and black salt (sanchal) for an interesting variation.

⚊ Raw Mango and Onion Chutney ⚊

A chutney with raw mango and onion may surprise you, but making this a part of your daily diet helps to prevent you from sunstrokes.

Preparation time : 10 minutes.   No cooking.   Makes 1 cup.

½ cup grated raw mango
½ cup grated white onions
2 tbsp grated jaggery (gur)
¼ tsp black salt (sanchal)
¼ tsp roasted cumin seed (jeera) powder
¼ tsp chilli powder
salt to taste

1. Mix all the ingredients in a bowl.
2. Keep aside till the jaggery melts.
3. Cover and keep refrigerate till required.
4. Relish this chutney with lunch everyday.

Handy tip : This lasts for upto 3 days if refrigerated but it's best to make it fresh everyday.